MARRIAGE:

PAST AND PRESENT

EXTENDING HORIZONS BOOKS

TOYNBEE AND HISTORY: Critical Essays and Reviews
edited by M. F. Ashley Montagu

MUTUAL AID: A Factor of Evolution, by Petr Kropotkin

MARRIAGE: PAST AND PRESENT, by Robert Briffault and
Bronislaw Malinowski

THE AMERICAN SEX REVOLUTION, by Pitirim Sorokin

MARRIAGE: PAST AND PRESENT

A Debate Between

ROBERT BRIFFAULT

AND

BRONISLAW MALINOWSKI

Edited with an Introduction

By

M. F. ASHLEY MONTAGU

PORTER SARGENT PUBLISHER
Boston

CONTENTS

BIBLIOGRAPHIC NOTE

The six chapters which make up the present volume were delivered as a series of broadcasts over the British Broadcasting Corporation. They were simultaneously published in the official journal of the B.B.C., *The Listener* (London) in the six weekly issues beginning on 7 January 1931 and terminating with the issue of 11 February 1931. The talks are reprinted here for the first time. Two words which in their English context are quite inoffensive have been changed to their acceptable American forms. One of the same words has been dropped because of redundancy. These changes were made in chapter four. For the rest, the chapters stand exactly as they were printed in *The Listener*, to which journal thanks are due for having made them available.

The text is reprinted here through the courtesy of the editor of *The Listener* and the British Broadcasting Corporation.

ASHLEY
MONTAGU

ASHLEY
MONTAGU

INTRODUCTION

In 1927 Robert Briffault's three-volume work *The Mothers* was published. I read this enormous work in January 1930 and found it interesting, powerfully irritating, bold, challenging, often wrongheaded, and well-peppered with what appeared to me as original insights. The author, in addition to being an extraordinarily well-informed and industrious researcher, was also clearly a man of wit and style. Whatever one thought of his main thesis, one could not but help admire his artistry. Briffault's literary manners were something else again.[1] I had been a student of several of the authorities who appeared to be Briffault's particular black beasts. The anthropologist who was the victim of Briffault's severest criticism was referred to in a manner which can perhaps best be described as a combination of insinuation and innuendo. Since something of both the injustice and the flavour of Briffault's polemical writing is typically exemplified by the reference I have in mind, I had better quote it in Briffault's own words.

The views of Father Lafitau have, however, been revived by a Finnish writer who was introduced to the English public by Alfred Wallace, one of the authors of the theory of natural selection. Dr. Wallace entertained, among other peculiar views, the opinion that the law of evolution, while applying to all other forms of life, did not extend to the human race, which he regarded as the product of a special creation. Edward Westermarck, Dr. Wallace's protégé, taking little note of the discoveries of the founders of scientific anthropology concerning the principles of primitive social organization, "boldly challenged the conclusions of our most esteemed writers," and "arrived at different, and sometimes diametrically opposite, conclusions."[2] That revival of the doctrines of the seventeenth century Jesuit theologians was set forth by Dr. Westermarck with an industry in the collection of biographical references which outdid that of all previous writers, and with a dialectical adroitness not unworthy of the reputation of his noted predecessors.

And so on at great length. What Briffault, in fact, accused Westermarck of was the equivalent of selling stock in a nonexistent oil well. Briffault, in effect, accused Westermarck of dishonesty. This, to anyone who knew Westermarck, was a preposterous charge.[3] I felt that Briffault had done Westermarck a great injustice. Since he also aimed several undeserved shafts at another of my teachers, Bronislaw Malinowski, with whom I was then still working, I felt impelled to do something toward correcting Briffault's unfortunate misjudgement. Since, also, in reading Briffault's own astonishing *tour de force* it had seemed to me that he had not been clearly understood, in that he had been saddled with the view that Motherright was at one time the universal institution, whereas I had read him as principally attempting to prove that the nature of many human institutions was largely influenced by the functions of motherhood, I decided to put things straight, if I could, with Briffault. I therefore wrote him inquiring as to the correctness of my judgment of his thesis, and at the same time indicated to him how seriously he had misjudged Westermarck. Since Briffault's reply is not without some interest, I reproduce it here. It is dated 4 February 1930.

Dear Sir,

Thank you for your letter. You are quite right in not identifying my views with the conception of "Mother-right," which I have expressly disclaimed. In an abridged edition of *The Mothers* which will appear shortly I have avoided some sources of misunderstanding which, it seems, I did not take sufficiently into account in the first edition.

I am glad of what you say about Westermarck. I have not met him, but from what I have heard he must have a charming personality. I feel no animosity whatever towards him, but cannot help feeling some distress at the attitude of the scientific public generally in England which has accepted him so tamely. I like to think that he is incapable of a dishonest motive. The worst of it is that one cannot charge him with ignorance. How then is one to explain, for example, his account of the Igorots (*The Mothers,* ii, pp. 49 sqq.)? Such instances present an interesting psychological problem.

I am too busy at present to go out too much, but I shall be very pleased to see you at any time you would care to come. Could you come to tea next Tuesday (11th)?

Yours sincerely,

Robert Briffault.

In those days I kept a journal, and there is a full record in it of my visit to Briffault. I arrived at 4:30 for tea and, like the man who stayed to dinner, did not depart until 11:30 that night! It was the beginning of a friendship which lasted until Briffault's death in 1948.

After several visits with Briffault I suggested that he ought to meet Westermarck and Malinowski. In time a meeting was arranged, Westermarck inviting Briffault and his wife to tea at The London School of Economics. The tea took place on the 30th April 1930. I introduced the Briffaults to Westermarck, Malinowski, and Morris Ginsberg. Differences were reconciled, and Briffault was invited to present a paper at Westermarck's seminar the following week. This Briffault did on the 7th of May. It is recorded in my diary that it was excellent, but what it was about I failed to record, nor can I now remember. After the seminar there was tea once more in the Senior Common Room, with Malinowski, Westermarck, Ginsberg, the Briffaults, and myself attending.

Malinowski was much taken by Briffault. In many respects their personalities were not unlike. Both were Europeans rather than nationals in any narrow sense, they were urbane, witty, and *bon vivants*. Both spoke half a dozen European languages with ease, and they were interested in the same subject. They liked each other. Malinowski, as he told me, was going to see what he could do by way of helping Briffault to some permanent berth. One of the first things to develop this way was a series of broadcasts over the B.B.C. which Malinowski had been invited to give. He had suggested that Briffault also be invited to participate, and the suggestion had been adopted. And this is how what might have been a beautiful and enduring friendship came to an end. Malinowski and Briffault prepared their talks in manuscript and submitted them to each other. Discussions followed which became increasingly more acrimonious, so that by the time the seventh talk in the series was to be given, which was to have been a discussion between Malinowski and Briffault, and after literally some two dozen drafts of it had been made, the final "debate" was abandoned. This explains why the final two talks, in the series of six here reprinted, are by Malinowski, and why Briffault is not represented by a "last word." Ours is the loss, as theirs was, too. It would have been valuable to have the joint summing-up by Malinowski and Briffault, and it would have been so much more pleasing had they remained friends. But it was not to be.

Were it not for the fact that Mrs. Briffault had sent me copies of *The Listener*, the official publication of the British Broadcasting Company, in which the broadcasts were published immediately after they were made, I should probably never have known that they had been printed. Malinowski had told me in 1936 some of the details of his quarrel with Briffault over these broadcasts, but I don't recall that he referred to their publication. Since I already knew of their publication the point is not important. I mention the matter here only because these six most interesting printed broadcasts might have fallen into a bottomless pit so far as their being remembered is concerned. Only recently I had to draw their existence to the attention of a bibliographer of Malinowski's writings who had omitted nothing but these broadcasts from his list.

After twenty-five years this discussion of "Marriage: Past and Present", as the broadcast series was originally entitled, is for the first time reprinted and appears for the first time in book form in the present edition.

Since the original publication of these six broadcasts in *The Listener* twenty-five year ago, much research has been done on marriage by social scientists, and many changes have occurred in the *mores* of the civilized peoples of the world. To what extent does this great body of social research in any way affect the conclusions of Malinowski and Briffault? How have the social changes which since 1931 have taken place on so widespread a scale, virtually throughout the world, affected the institution of marriage in the light of Malinowski's and Briffault's discussion? How do the contributions of each of these workers measure up against the findings of contemporary social science, and especially of anthropology?

Since in what follows I propose to attempt something of an answer to these questions, the reader who desires to enjoy Malinowski and Briffault unbecommentated is advised to stop reading here, and go straight to the text itself. After he has

read that, he can return to the following section of this Introduction for the answers to the above questions.

* * * *

Malinowski's references to marriage and divorce in the
Soviet Union are unusually interesting in the light of the re-
visions in the direction of "bourgeois" practices which the Communists have had to make. Even before 1931 the Communists
had been forced to return to a "bourgeois" conception of the
family; and they were soon to discover that since, as in all
societies, the family is based on marriage, it is impossible to
play tricks with the one without affecting the other. The Communists, being essentially men of blueprints and Five-Year Economic Plans, committed the error of trying to put economic
planning before human relations. It is impossible to put economics before human relations for the simple reason that economics is a function of human relations—and not the other
way around, as the Communists were to discover from their
own experience. Malinowski points out how nineteenth-century
reformers and enthusiastic socialists "preached free love and
sexual communism by reference to the ape and his matrimonial
entanglements." Such thinkers were largely influenced by the
anecdotal anthropology of their day, and there can be not the
least doubt that, as Malinowski states, it also greatly influenced
the planning of the Soviet State. Karl Marx was himself deeply
read in that literature, as was Engels. One has but to recall the
writings of Charles Letourneau, who wrote one book on *The
Evolution of Marriage* and another on *Property,* the writings
of the brothers Elie and Jacques Reclus, Karl Kautsky, Kropotkin, and numerous others all either in the anarchist or communist tradition, to realize how deeply influenced these social
revolutionaries were by the primitive anthropology of their
day. It is not surprising to find that the Communists, even in
the second half of the twentieth century, largely disregard the
findings of twentieth century social anthropology and cleave to
those of the nineteenth century. A fascinating book begs to

be written on the relation between nineteenth century anthropology and the Communist conception of human social institutions. Not all, but a good deal of nineteenth-century anthropology was half-baked. Its theoretic implications were often unsoundly based, and the practices based on such theories were bound to end in failure. The Communists tried the experiment of collapsing the family and marriage, and found that neither the family nor marriage were, as *Pravda* had insisted, "personal matters." By 1946, marriage, divorce, and abortion were returned to the jurisdiction of the State, and were no longer at the personal discretion of anyone. Family limitation is no longer the mode, but large families are now actively encouraged by monetary and other material awards. The Communists have been forced to accept some of the irreducible facts of life.

In Italy divorce is again legal, and the Draconic penalties once attached to birth control by Mussolini have been removed. Professor J. B. Watson, with his statement that "In fifty years there will be no such thing as marriage", has once again been proved profoundly wrongheaded. If there is one thing we can be certain of as anthropologists, it is that marriage will endure as long as human society endures. There is no society known to anthropologists without the institution of marriage, and it is highly improbable that there could ever be such a society.

To the prophets of family doom Malinowski's simple answer "rubbish," is still the most appropriate reply—as it will always be. After a quarter of a century—a very short time in the history of mankind—anthropologists fully subscribe to Malinowski's conclusion "that marriage and the family always have been, are, and will remain the foundations of human society." Never was a scientist's prediction more fully realized than Malinowski's words in his final talk: "The reforms of Fascist Italy and of Soviet Russia alike will, I am convinced, lead to the same result: a return to the old order of marriage and family based neither on absolute freedom nor on complete and rigid compulsion."

Briffault's criticism of patriarchal marriage was a most valuable one when it was made, and one would like to think that it played some part, if not perhaps as great a role as A. P. Herbert's novel *Holy Deadlock* (1934), in influencing legislative opinion in the direction of liberalizing the marriage and divorce laws of England. Whether, in fact, Briffault's trenchant criticism, made here and elsewhere in his writings, of marriage laws weighted in favour of the male had any effect upon legislation I do not know. The tracing of such relationships is not always possible, but if words do influence conduct one cannot help but think that somewhere in the minds of some English legislators Briffault's words may have had a reverberative effect.

In reading Briffault it is necessary to remember that he was pleading a special case, namely, the matriarchal theory of social evolution. Briffault had arrived at this theory quite independently of his much earlier predecessors in that theory Bachofen (1861) and McLennan (1865). In the Preface to *The Mothers* (1927) Briffault tells us how he arrived at the theory.

> I had proposed to draw up a list of the forms of the social instincts, and to investigate their origin. I had not proceeded far before I discovered, to my surprise, that the social characters of the human mind are, one and all, traceable to the operation of instincts that are related to the functions of the female and not to those of the male. That the mind of women should have exercised so fundamental an influence upon human development in the conditions of historical patriarchal societies, is inconceivable. I was thus led to reconsider the early development of human society, of its fundamental institutions and traditions, in the light of the matriarchal theory of social evolution.

Briffault's whole thesis is stated in these words. He explicitly rejected the view that there had ever been any society in which women ruled as the dominant sex; by "matriarchy" he meant that in earlier societies the interests, desires, and functions of women played a much more important role than they are permitted or acknowledged to do in civilized societies, and that women had influenced the social organization of human societies very much more considerably than was generally understood or admitted.[4]

As I have said, Briffault was a special pleader, and this greatly mars the presentation of his case in *The Mothers*. The same fault is apparent in his debate with Malinowski. Furthermore Briffault is often inaccurate, as will be apparent from the notes at the end of this volume. Briffault was one of the most erudite men of his time, and at the same time a man of violent enthusiasms. When he became enamoured of a viewpoint nothing could stop him, and like a river in flood he would carry everything before him. Unlike Malinowski he was not a scientist. He was a brilliant, and often prejudiced, thinker. The one element in scientific work that Briffault did not understand is that the good scientist, when he becomes enamoured of a theory, not only sets out to collect the evidence which will support it, but as zealously seeks for any and all evidence which will refute it. Briffault did not fail to deal with the evidence that was opposed to his theory, but he was convinced from the beginning that such evidence, since it did not fit his theory, must be wrong, and so he attempted to dismiss it—only too frequently by arguments *ad hominem*. It is the greatest pity, because the combination of his literary manners and his special pleading repelled many of his readers.

In the two essays and the debate with Malinowski by which he is represented here, Briffault is in quieter voice, though the special pleading is still evident. What was, in part at least, behind Briffault's enlistment in the cause of matriarchy was his abhorrence of injustice, and in this case the injustices practised by men upon women. He was not a feminist, but he felt, as he wrote in the final words of the one-volume edition of *The Mothers* that "The practical lesson which the true history of the relations between the sexes does seem to point is that mutual co-operation between them and social equality are more conducive to the smooth working of social organisation than any form of sex antagonism." It is partly in the light of this belief of Briffault's that his contributions here reprinted should be read.[5]

The crucial chapter in this book is the third in which Malinowski and Briffault debate the question "What is a Family?" It is here that the differences between scientific anthropology as represented by Malinowski and the clever theorising of the library-anthropologist as represented by Briffault are clearly brought out. This chapter alone would have made the book worth publishing. The issues between the two schools are here seen more sharply and succinctly presented than one would be able to find anywhere else in the whole realm of anthropological literature. What is the original nature of the family? Was group-marriage ever a reality? What is the meaning of polygamy? What, in fact, is marriage? Was sexual communism ever a reality? The answers to these questions are brilliantly illuminated in this memorable discussion, and it may be recorded that contemporary anthropology is completely on the side of Malinowski and against Briffault. Group-marriage and sexual promiscuity as cultural institutions have long since been relegated to the Museum of Anthropological Curiosities.[6] If the facts have gone against Briffault, however, we nonetheless remain grateful to him for putting the case for the matriarchal school of social evolution so clearly.

Briffault, in chapter four "The Business Side of Marriage," makes several assertions which are unwarranted by the facts. Similar assertions have often been made by other writers on this subject. The first is "that in every quarter of the globe and in every age" the transaction of marriage "rests chiefly, and in most instances exclusively, upon economic considerations." The second is that romantic love is absent among "savages." In emphasizing the sacramental nature of marriage in chapter five Malinowski provides the proper emphasis, and by implication denies the validity of Briffault's suggestion that "in the lower stages of society" marriage is an economic transaction. It is, indeed, doubtful whether there are any societies in which marriage rests either chiefly or exclusively upon economic considerations. Briffault's statement to this effect is typical of his method, when it pleases his fancy, to take a part for the whole. Furthermore, it is wholly to misunderstand the nature and meaning of the transactions involved.

When, for example, a groom among the peoples of East Africa makes a gift of cattle to his future father-in-law, the gift represents something vastly more than, and significantly different from, a "payment" to the father for the loss of the economic services of his daughter. The gift is made as a social means of regularising a relationship between a man and a woman who by their union will involve two extended families and almost certainly two clans. The cattle and other gifts are actually contributed by the members of the extended family of the groom. Such gifts are in turn redistributed by the bride's father to his relatives, perhaps those who on a former occasion helped him gather the cattle which made possible the marriage of his own son. The recipients of the gifts thus widely distributed among the relatives at the time of the marriage become more than ever responsibly involved in maintaining the stability of the marriage. Those who participate in a dowry tend to have certain obligations to the married couple and their children. The "bride-wealth" (or "brideprice") functions as a socially stabilizing mechanism, such economic effects as it may have being purely secondary to this. By its payment a wife is not purchased, and she does not become her husband's property or chattel.[7]

As for Briffault's denial of the existence of romantic love among "savages," Malinowski, in the fifth chapter, has sufficiently made the proper risposte. Both in *The Mothers* and in his book *Les Troubadours et le Sentiment Romanesque* (1945) Briffault attempted to show that the concept of romantic love was a late development of civilized societies. This is largely true, but it does not follow that therefore romantic love does not exist in uncivilized societies. Anthropologists know only too well that in many respects civilized societies have a great deal to learn that is "advanced" from so-called "primitive" societies. In the sense in which we often misguidedly think of the non-literate peoples of the earth as "primitive," there are none, in many respects, so primitive as the civilized. All anthropologists are evolutionists, but Briffault was an orthogenist, a straight-line evolutionist, so that if a trait was found to be a late development in civilized society that fact constituted *prima facie* evidence for Briffault that it could not have existed in a primitive or non-literate society. The concept of reticulate evolution was unknown to Briffault. This orthogenism combined with his particular prejudices made it impossible for him to interpret the evidence correctly.

It is refreshing to find Briffault saying, "Human beings are, I firmly believe, naturally sympathetic, affectionate, and kind hearted." Such scientific evidence as bears upon this statement which has accumulated during the last quarter of a century fully supports that dictum.[8] In the Age of the Atom Bomb and the Death Instinct, however, this view is having a hard time getting itself established.

Briffault's leaning toward communism was either the cause or the effect of his tendency to see all human institutions as having been economically determined. It is not surprising, therefore, to find him asserting that "The patriarchal privileges which modern women are disposed to resent are founded in the last resort upon economic advantages." And he goes on to add that "They are not founded upon the possession by men of superior physical force or superior brains, but in the possession of a superior banking account."

This is the equivalent of saying that the privileges of the French in Algeria and of the British in India were founded not on the possession by these colonial powers of superior physical strength, but in the last resort upon economic advantage. Could any argument be sillier than that? Of course the economic advantages were there, but it was superior physical strength that made them possible for the colonial powers, just as it is greater muscular power which has enabled the male throughout history to enforce his will upon the female. Of course women have been economically dependent upon men in many cultures, but that economic dependence is brought about by many other factors in addition to the male's greater muscular power. The division of labour between the sexes in all societies, and the fact that women bear, nurse, and care for children tends to make the female more sedentary than the male. Under certain conditions she can be encouraged to become largely dependent upon the male for her sustenance—but this is by no means the case in all societies. In non-literate societies, as a rule, both sexes must work in order to live, and that necessity to work has nothing whatever to do with the patriarchal or matriarchal structure of society. It is no argument whatever to say that because women in non-literate societies are not as economically dependent upon men as are women in modern patriarchal societies, therefore patriarchal society cannot be supposed to represent the primeval condition of the human race. It is greatly to be doubted whether human societies were ever universally one thing or the other. They are not so now and it is unlikely that they ever were.

Briffault's hope that marriage will become "more and more a private contract" is an overintellectualized hope which rather sadly reveals how little he really understood of the meaning of society. It is the greatest error to conceive of marriage as a matter of private interest. A couple may be attracted toward each other and marry for purely personal reasons, in short, because they are in love. But the contract they make with each other at marriage involves far more than their private selves. Every marriage immediately involves two or four extended families. There may also be involved different ethnic, religious, social, and other groups. And intelligence and justice lies in realizing that marriage is not merely a private affair between two persons but that it consists, in addition, in the creation of many new extended relationships and responsibilities. One doesn't simply marry a person, one marries into that person's family. This being so, no marriage can with intelligence and justice, ever be conceived as a private agreement between two persons. The State also has an interest in every marriage, and that interest consists in more than simply supplying a marriage certificate.

The families related thus by marriage and the State enter into the agreement. While quite true as far as it goes it is an unintentional oversimplification to say, as Malinowski does, that "marriage is a binding contract between one man and one woman for the establishment of an individual family." This was perhaps an unavoidable way of putting what Malinowski had to say in arguing the case against group marriage. That the State enters into the marriage agreement should be obvious, for without the sanction of the State there can be no marriage, nor can there be a dissolution of that marriage without its consent. In non-literate societies a marriage involves the 'marrying families' in all sorts of new relationships and obligations, prescribed and regulated vis-a-vis each of the members of the 'marrying families.' There are, for example, the elaborate mother-in-law and other avoidance relationships, maternal avuncular obligations, cross-cousin relationships, affinal relationships, sexual prohibitions, and the like.[9] The importance, in addition, of religious sanctions need not be dealt with here, as they have been sufficiently emphasized by Malinowski in chapter five.

In our own time, in the Western World, marriage is rapidly losing its religious character, and increasingly tends to become a secular arrangement. Even the solemnities of a church service have tended to become secularized, being often made the occasion for conspicuous consumption and much-valued publicity. What was at one time a religious service is often turned into a stage-managed performance. The forms are maintained, but they have been emptied of virtually all their original meaning, as is borne out by the fact that many couples without any religious affiliation whatever will go through all the motions of a church wedding because it is considered *socially* the thing to do. Increasing numbers of marriages, in this and the other sense, are celebrated outside the church. To those for whom science has become the secular religion of the day, Malinowski, far from urging the abandonment of the sacrament of marriage, on the contrary shows that the institution of marriage and the family can be endowed with new values which can render their stability and sacredness as great as they have ever been.

ASHLEY MONTAGU

Malinowski's summing-up in the sixth chapter puts the case as clearly as could be for marriage always having been an individual arrangement as opposed to marriage as or between groups. The conclusions of contemporary anthropologists on the matter are resumed in the words of Murdock, "In fine, there is no evidence that group marriage anywhere exists, or ever has existed, as the prevailing type of marital union." [10]

Amusingly enough while Briffault, as Malinowski says, was unwilling to affirm the existence of group-maternity—and quite rightly—the phenomenon has actually been shown to exist in at least one human society, namely, among the Kaingang of Brazil.[11] Among the Kaingang the co-spouses are either siblings or first cousins, and the children of a man's wives regard the latter as their mothers. But it must also be pointed out that in the same society the children of a woman's husbands regard the latter as their fathers. Group maternity is no more the rule in this society than is group paternity; both co-exist. The evidence indicates fairly clearly that the Kaingang are a society in state of dissolution, and in no way can be taken as typical of anything other than themselves.

Malinowski asks the question: "Will women give over their infants into the hands of the State to be brought up as foundlings or communal babies?" The crêches of the Communists have gone, but in Israel a new experiment has come into being, namely the *kibbutz*. In the kibbutz the working parents leave their children for the greater part of the day in charge of a competent personnel. The arrangement is a community one, and it seems to work very well. The kibbutz, however, is not intended to be a substitute for the family, but a means of taking care of children while the parents are away during the working day.[12] Such experiments are interesting, and in Israel represent the solution of a difficult problem, but they no more suggest the direction in which the family is developing than a refugee camp constitutes a pattern for the permanent status of humanity. Kibbutzim, crêches, and refugee camps constitute temporary devices pending the return to normal conditions. The biologically normal state of the basic human biologic group is the family, consisting of parents and their children, and we can be quite certain that nothing will ever permanently change that fact. Since the family is based upon marriage it is similarly possible to predict the permanence of that institution. And this is what Malinowski does in the last of the talks printed in this volume.

During the quarter of a century which has elapsed since this debate on "The Future of Marriage" took place between Briffault and Malinowski the status of women in many parts of the world has markedly improved. The increasing political and social freedoms which women enjoy have greatly, and beneficially, affected the institution of marriage. The marriage service no longer requires women "to obey" their husbands; and husbands on the whole, it is generally agreed, are the better for the improvement in the status of their wives. In spite of rising divorce rates and broken families, marriage and family relationships have undergone fundamental changes for the better. With the increasing freedoms which both sexes are reciprocally enjoying, and the recognition of the rights and sanctity of the individual regardless of sex or other group membership, there has occurred an improved understanding of the meaning of marriage and the family.

The general increase in divorce rates is not to be regarded as an evidence of the breakdown of marriage, but may be looked upon rather as a symptom of the adjustment to a world of values which are in transition from the old to the new. The new freedoms have brought with them increased responsibilities; and freedom itself (as witnessed by the democratic process) is a responsibility which it takes time to learn. The high rates of divorce are but an evidence of the increased freedom of the individual, and freedom is a good thing, and so are many of the divorces between persons who should never have married in the first place. The prolongation of a marriage which has failed is destructive to all concerned—especially from the point of view of the children, whose happiness and fulfilment is all important. There are also some divorces which should never have occurred.[13]

What we have learned during the last twenty-five years is that we have to do more than we have in the past towards preparing young people for marriage in a relationship which today demands more understanding than was ever before necessary. At the same time we need to do what requires to be done towards the education of adults in the meaning of marriage—its problems, challenges, and rewards. In these matters the young will always learn most from the adults upon whom they model themselves—and such models are best provided by the parents.

Happily, in the western world, there are many evidences that the problems of marriage in a world in transition are receiving increasingly serious attention. There are today marriage councils, marriage counselors, experts, journals, syndicated columns, articles, books, radio and television programs—where formerly there were none—all devoted to assisting the individual to arrive at a better understanding of the nature and meaning of marriage. The problems of marriage are now for the first time receiving the benefit of scientific study. The expectation may legitimately be entertained that as a result of the multiplication of such activities marriage is likely to become more stable and divorces fewer than they have been in the recent past and are at present. Towards this end the present volume may be offered as a small contribution.

Princeton, N. J.   M. F. Ashley Montagu

BRONISLAW
MALINOWSKI

BRONISLAW
MALINOWSKI

CHAPTER I

THE PRESENT CRISIS IN MARRIAGE

Within the last generation or two the conditions of
life have undergone profound and revolutionary changes.
We are all feeling that we have been thrown into a new
world, and not a very comfortable world at that. Whither
are we moving? In which direction are we going to be
driven? Even in the last anchorage of peace, even in our
own home, we seem to be threatened.

What is the present situation as regards marriage
and the family? Traditional morals and the legal framework of domestic life are undergoing disquieting changes.
There is a crisis in marriage and there is a great deal of
noise about it. Let me add at once for your comfort that
there is more of the noise than of the crisis. But there

is some substance in the view that family and marriage are becoming modified; that they are threatened by certain influences; and that wise reforms are needed in order to safeguard their future.

Let us have a look at the facts all around us. Most startling of all, we have, in Soviet Russia, revolutionary experiments on a vast scale. Here a number of remarkable enactments have modified the juridical character of marriage almost out of recognition. Marriage, in the eyes of the law, has completely ceased to be a religious institution. It has almost ceased to be a legal contract. It is regarded as a sociological fact. Marriage comes into being when two people of opposite sex decide to live together, to share a household, to co-operate economically. The registration of marriage is not a creative act which constitutes a legal reality. It is merely a proof of its existence. Nor is this proof indispensable. Divorce, again—or, as it is called in Soviet Russia, the cessation of marriage—takes place when the two consorts actually separate. This may be registered, but need not be so. Marriage ceases to exist *when* it ceases to exist.

WHERE 'GROUP MARRIAGE' IS POSSIBLE

Communist marriage is thus, in the eyes of the law, a perfectly free and voluntary arrangement. Adultery is not a legal offence. Bigamy is not punishable by law. In juridical theory it is, therefore, possible in Soviet Russia to establish what the sociologist calls 'group marriages' or communal unions. That is to say, several men and several women may run a communal household, and indiscriminately share as much of their lives as they like.

Sensational as this idea seems, and novel and daring as the experiment might appear in a young and revolutionary society, group marriage is a very old and, to the anthropologist, a familiar concept. Many a learned student of human history believes that man started his matrimonial career without the institutions of monogamy or individual marriage—groups of people mating with other groups, and producing children who did not recognise any individual parents and who were communally tended and nurtured. Some revolutionary reformers, notably the enthusiastic German socialists of the nineteenth century, preached free love and sexual communism by reference to the ape man and his matrimonial entanglements. These writers have, in fact, influenced modern Russian theory and practice, and here you see how anthropology has affected, not to say misguided, practical affairs. I, personally, speaking as an anthropologist, do not for one moment admit that group marriage has ever been practised in any human society however primitive, nor do I believe that marriage and family life will degenerate to any appreciable degree in modern Russia, in spite of any legal opportunities and loopholes. But there are eminent scholars even now who assume that group marriage was the early form of mating.

LIFE AND LEGAL LOOPHOLES

Returning to Russia, the deepest changes have been brought about in the Soviet home by the legal dissociation of kinship and marriage. There the relations of mother and father to children are based on parenthood, and not on the contract of marriage. Illegitimate children are, therefore, set on the same footing as those born in wedlock; and a dissolution of marriage does not alter their legal relations to father and mother respectively.

If I were to add that Soviet law fully allows, not to say encourages, all practices of family limitation, that is, has made abortion legal, that there are no punishments for incest, some of you might be disgusted and scandalised, others, perhaps very enthusiastic. But please do not allow your emotions and your political views or sympathies to interfere with your dispassionate interest in these facts. I want to rule out all political bias and all moral judgment. What we are after are the facts and a clear understanding of them. And in this it is by no means easy to assess rightly what is happening in Russia. We must remember two things: first of all, that what I have described to you is the letter of the law, and not the facts of life, and these two do not always coincide. In the second place — and this is even more important — you must remember that in human society, as in nature generally, it is impossible to foretell the results of an experiment — except by making the experiment and watching the results.

We hear that present-day Russians are abolishing the church wedding and the legal contract of marriage. Is this such a tremendous revolution? Nothing of the sort. Marriage without any contractual act is even nowadays practised in Scotland, a country not obsessed by the spirit of communism. It is also allowed in several States of North America, and it was approved by canonical law right through the Middle Ages up till the Council of Trent.

Take the facility of divorce, again. Does it make marriage completely nugatory? In Ancient Rome repudiation even by one consort legally made an end to the union. The repudiation by the husband of the wife is the accepted form of terminating an orthodox Jewish marriage. And, as we shall see from the subsequent discussion, the facility of divorce does not seriously upset marriage, for its stability does not rest upon legal compulsion only. The difficulty thus consists in understanding what the foundations of family and marriage really are. And it is here that the comparative study of marriage in primitive and civilised societies alike can help us.

MARRIAGE 'REFORMS'

I chose the most sensational example of legislative experiment to show you under the magnifying-glass of revolutionary reform the difficulties of the problem in assessing what certain changes really mean. I might have taken the reforms of Fascist Italy, which have, one and all, the opposite intention — that of strengthening marriage and the family. In Italy divorce has now been made illegal. Draconic penalties are attached to any attempt mechanically or surgically to limit the number of children. The whole institution has been placed very much under the control of the Roman Catholic Church and of the State. We might have considered equally Turkey, India, or the United States. In all such cases, whether we feel appalled or enthusiastic about the reforms, we should like to know what are the guarantees of the future; what can the sociologist forecast? Nor is it only the vast legislative experiments which might well make us feel profoundly anxious. All around us we see signs more or less significant and disquieting. To most people marriage has always been rooted in religion and morality. At present, however, the general trend seems to be towards a civil conception of marriage. Among other consequences, this affords greater facilities for divorce.

ECONOMIC FACTORS

Take domestic morality, again. Two elements exercise a far-reaching influence — the economic independence of woman and the mechanical means of fertility-control. Even a generation ago, the daughter was sheltered by her home and the wife remained under the supervision of her husband. Today, a woman demands freedom and independence, and she must have it in order to contribute her economic quota to the household. It is impossible to supervise her; the double standard of morality must go. Either man must allow his mate the same freedom as he has always been granted; or else we must base a new charter of strict conduct for both sexes alike on mutual trust, respect, and understanding. Economically, again, the household is not what it used to be. What with the difficulty of domestic service, the facilities of joint kitchens and dining-rooms, the home is no more the only place of convivial reunion.

In the nursery, also, things appear somewhat gloomy. Childbirth, from a ceremonial and essentially domestic event, is rapidly becoming a clinical fact. Among the working classes, the infant has often to be taken away from the mother soon after weaning or even before. The State subventioned and controlled school is to a large extent replacing the educational and moral influences which, up till recently, were vested exclusively in the family.

Is The Family Doomed?

All these facts are certainly disquieting. One and all raise the question: is this a symptom of a deadly disease in our body politic; is this an indication of the downfall of the family and marriage? The prophets are not wanting. 'In fifty years there will be no such thing as marriage'. So speaks Professor J. B. Watson, the founder and leader of the Behaviorist School. Lesser lights join the chorus and vociferously frame an indictment of the family and prophesy its proximate disappearance. Listen to the chorus: 'The home is illimitably selfish, psychologically egocentric, spiritually dwarfish and decivilizing'. And again: 'The family is unnatural'. And again: 'The family is the factory of feeble-mindedness and insanity'. And the moral: 'The family must go; the sooner the better'. All these are quotations from the chorus of what we might call 'misbehaviourists'. 'Misbehaviourism' is the label which I like to affix to this group of noisy, amusing, and aggressive publicists. The brief answer to all such theories and views is — 'rubbish'.

THE PRESENT CRISIS IN MARRIAGE

Marriage and the family are undergoing a change, nay, passing through a crisis. To close your eyes to it, to say that all is for the best in the best of matrimonial worlds, would be as shallow and as unscientific as to prophesy the downfall of the family. Some changes are necessary; but these will not affect the essential constitution of the family.

I think we shall have to establish a single standard of morality, a greater legal and economic equality of husband and wife, much greater freedom in parental relations and a greater tolerance of children towards their parents. But all this will leave the family and marriage conspicuously unaltered, in spite of all the din and dust of controversy. Why, what is the moral to be drawn even from Soviet Russia? The plain fact is that family life seems to be going on there steadily and happily; that marriages are entered upon and that they are carried on satisfactorily. Do they divorce twice a day? On the contrary, they live for years in satisfactory unions. There is something bigger in human marriage and the family than the legal framework by which it is usually bound together.

Why do I so confidently affirm the strength and permanence of marriage and family? Because my conviction is derived from the scientific study of the two institutions, extended over the widest compass of human experience, that embraced by anthropology. This science teaches us, that marriage and the family are rooted in the deepest needs of human nature and society; that they are associated with progress, spiritual and material.

The real task of anthropology consists in giving us insight into the essentials of marriage and the family, as well as the understanding of their value for society. Many a student of man still strains his imagination in order to visualize the beginnings of human marriage, in order to diagnose how original man or his ancestor, the ape, mated. And then this is set up for our imitation. The hunt for origins and their use as a precedent is an unprofitable but, unfortunately, only too common manner of using anthropological evidence.

I shall not argue, therefore, that modern marriage is valuable because the chimpanzee practised strict monogamy. I shall, however, in the course of these talks, prove to the best of my ability that marriage and the family always have been, are, and will remain the foundations of human society.

ROBERT
BRIFFAULT

ROBERT
BRIFFAULT

CHAPTER II

THE ORIGINS OF PATRIARCHAL

MARRIAGE

Professor Malinowski reminded you last week that our marriage institutions have come in of late for a good deal of criticism. He mentioned some of the causes of that matrimonial unrest. I shall refer to one only, not the least in importance. The criticism comes not from the East or from the West, from Bolshevists or from American misbehaviourists. It comes chiefly from the women of England. It is called forth by certain features of our marriage institutions which, while they make husband and wife one, seem to provide that the husband shall be that one. The subordinate position of the wife is indicated by her vow of obedience, by the legal and economic disabilities under which she labours, by her obligation to assume, not only her husband's name, but to set aside her very nationality and assume his.

Those and similar features of our institutions constitute the patriarchal conception of the marriage relation. That conception can be traced in the history of culture. It is embodied, as you know, in the Pauline doctrine. 'Wives,' says the Apostle, 'submit yourselves unto your husbands as unto the Lord. Let the wives be subject to their husbands in everything. Let them be discreet, chaste, let them stay at home and obey their husbands.' Ancient ecclesiastical law authorized a man to enforce those principles by beating his wife with a whip. Those patriarchal principles were largely taken over by the early Church from Greek and Roman usage. The poet Menander speaks in almost the same terms as St. Paul. 'Silence, modesty, and to stay quietly at home,' he says, 'are the most becoming virtues in a wife.' Roman tradition was, you know, strenuously patriarchal. 'Our fathers,' said the elder Cato, 'have willed that women should be in the power of their fathers, of their brothers, of their husbands. Our fathers have bound down women by law, and bent them to their power.' Roman tradition was exactly similar to that of the ancient Hindu. The laws of Manu laid down that, 'No act is to be done by a woman according to her will. She should worship her husband—even though he be of bad conduct, debauched, devoid of every quality —as if he were a god.'

Sir Henry Maine, the great authority of Victorian England on social history, taught that those patriarchal features of our institutions represent 'the primaeval condition of the human race,' and a school of anthropologists which has enjoyed great influence and popularity in England has expounded the same theory of social origins. The characteristic doctrine of that school is that, as things are now, so they have been from the beginning, and ever shall be. The question is not one of merely historical interest. The real question which the evidences of anthropology are called upon to elucidate is whether the sentiments with which existing institutions are regarded are part of human nature or are products of culture and social tradition.

PICK UP YOUR BLANKET AND BUDGE

If we survey the marriage usages of various peoples at all stages of culture, we find that they differ profoundly in many respects. The difference which in the light of our own tradition is most apt to attract attention is that, while among Christian nations monogamy is of the essence of the marriage relation, that principle is not recognised in Oriental or African cultures, or in fact in any of the lower phases of culture. It was indeed set down for the first time as a legal obligation during the sixth century of our era by the emperor Justinian.

But there are differences even more fundamental between the more primitive forms of marriage and those obtaining in advanced cultures. With most civilised peoples and many uncivilised ones the custom is, as with ourselves, for the wife to join her husband,

leaving her own people and her home, and to form a
new family of which the husband is the head. But we
find that among an enormous number of peoples in
the lower phases of culture that arrangement does not
occur. Instead of the wife joining her husband, the
husband joins the wife, who remains in her own home
and among her people. The women never leave the
social group in which they were born; their husbands
either come to live with them, or simply visit them.
That form of marriage is called *matrilocal*, as opposed
to our own *patrilocal* usage, and is found to be the
usual custom over four continents. It was the universal
native custom among all the races of the American con-
tinent, from the Eskimo of Baffin Bay to the Firelanders
of Cape Horn. Thus, for example, among the Indian
tribes of North America, 'the woman,' we are told,
'never leaves her home. The children belong to the
mother. The father takes up his abode with his mother-
in-law. No matter how many children he might have
in the house, he might at any time be ordered to pick
up his blanket and budge.' Or again, among the tribes
of the Orinoco, 'the women never follow their husbands,
but it is the husbands who follow their wives. From the
moment that a savage takes a wife, he no longer recog-
nises his own home. It is thus the fashion with all
savages that the sons go to other people's homes and
daughters remain in theirs'. The same custom is still
found among all races in Africa: among the Pygmies
of the Congo forests among whom the camps consist
of brothers and sisters, their wives and their husbands
living in some other camp; among the Bushmen, who
leave their own band and join that of their wives; among

the Bantus of Nyasaland and Kenya; in the Sudan, among the Tuareg of the Sahara. Altogether, the rule that women remain in their own home or group after marriage, and are joined by their husbands is the native custom of from one-third to one-half of the peoples of the uncivilised world,[1] allowing, of course, for the breaking up of all native customs in the last few decades by contact with Europeans, missionary and others, which greatly discounts the value of any investigation carried out at the present day.

BUYING A BRIDE

The further question arises, which is the older custom—for the wife to join the husband or for the husband to join the wife? In point of fact, wherever the patrilocal form of marriage obtains there is abundant evidence that the matrilocal usage obtained formerly:[2] whereas there is no evidence among the people who observe the matrilocal form of marriage that they ever had any other. The conclusion appears clear that the matrilocal form of marriage preceded the patrilocal, or patriarchal, form. The matter can be put to an exact test. Except in Christian countries, whenever a man removes his wife from her home and brings her to his, he has to make a payment for the right to do so. The transaction is often spoken of as purchasing a wife. But, except in some slave-holding countries, it is not regarded in that light. Long after the establishment of Christianity in northern Europe, the idea survived that a woman who had not been adequately paid for was not properly and respectably married. Among the

Christianised Negroes of South Africa at the present day payment of the bride-price is often made in secret, so as to satisfy the parties of the legality of the contract and of the legitimacy of the children. The payment is made in some form or other wherever the wife goes to live with her husband and becomes a member of his family. It is nowhere made where she does not join him. The payment, then, is made not to purchase a wife, but to purchase the right to remove her to her husband's home, in other words, to establish the patriarchal form of marriage. In many parts of the East Indies the native custom of matrilocal marriage obtains side by side with the patriarchal Islamic custom in the same community. When the latter is adopted, a payment must be made; when the native usage is adhered to, there is no question of payment. The arrangement with which we are familiar is thus a privilege originally acquired by paying for it.

THE WOMAN PAYS

It is, I think, obvious that where a woman remains in her own home and among her own people after marriage, the patriarchal principles embodied in our own institutions cannot be effectively enforced. It does not follow that the women lord it over the men. There are doubtless henpecked husbands and oppressed wives under any form of marriage. But the legal status of the wife who is joined in her own home by her husband cannot be the same as that of the wife who leaves her people and assumes her husband's name and nationality. And in fact, with the usage of matrilocal marriage are found associated a number of other usages which differ profoundly from those obtaining in patriarchal societies. Kinship and descent are reckoned in the female line exclusively;[3] fatherhood is left out of account. A child takes his mother's, not his father's, name. He belongs to her clan, not to the family of his father. The latter has no claim of any sort over the children. They do not inherit from him, but from their mother and from her brothers. Landed property is not vested in the men, but in the women.

Those conditions have given place to patriarchal institutions only where men have devised means of exchange or have acquired private property, notably in the form of cattle, which has enabled them to purchase those rights that have become part of the tradition of patriarchal civilisations. As Sir Henry Maine rightly stated, the pastoral societies pictured in Hebrew records present the type of patriarchal societies. But the pastoral societies in which men acquire by the payment of a bride-price the right which was denied to Jacob, to remove, even after twenty years, his wife and children to his own home, do not represent by a long way the primeval condition of the human race.

KNOW WHAT YOU'RE ABOUT

The great Puritan poet represented the first parents of mankind as perfectly patriarchal:

> For contemplation he and valour form'd
> For softness she and sweet attractive grace,
> He for God only, and she for God in him.

The poets and the popular anthropologists of a patriarchal society like Puritan or Victorian England like to
think of established institutions as 'the primeval condition of the human race.' The assumption did no
great harm so long as women accepted the established
tradition, and were content to be submissive, obedient,
and ignorant patriarchal wives. But the assumption of
Adam-and-Eve anthropology ceases to be harmless
when women are no longer content to derive resigna-
tion from its assurances. When they are protesting
against patriarchal principles, they are under the im-
pression that they are rebelling against the institution
of marriage, against that association and co-operation
of the sexes which lies at the root of all social culture
and of the sentiments of civilised humanity. In reality
they are doing nothing of the sort. They are raising
the protest of equity and common sense against traditional principles which are, historically speaking, of
late origin. That a man and a woman who are attracted to one another should agree to share life in
mutual devotion is one of the most satisfactory arrangements which social culture has brought into being. But
it is an arrangement the success of which is not provided
for by natural instincts. Above all, it is an arrangement
the success of which is not promoted by moral coercion,
by appeals to authority, by the dictatorship of tradition.
Those things are the very opposite of human affection.
Marriage is not helped but imperilled by assuming them.
When the husband, imbued with patriarchal principles,
having signed the legal contract in the vestry or regis-
ter office, considers that the woman's part of the bar-
gain, the dedication of her body, her love, her devotion

to him, the dissolution of her interests in his, must follow automatically by a natural law, as the result of eternal moral obligations, of dispositions dating from primeval humanity, he is being misled by what appears to me an erroneous and tendencious anthropology into the most tragic of disasters. Those apparently harmless edifying anthropological speculations are in a measure responsible for converting the most precious of social relations into the most tragic. The chief condition for the success of marriage is to know what one is about. To know the truth about social relations and institutions means to know their origin and history. You may perhaps now perceive why the unprejudiced study of anthropology, of the manners and customs of savages—a subject which may seem to you idle, boresome, and even repellent—has a most important bearing upon the deepest facts of life. You are all anthropologists, just as you are all prose writers and all metaphysicians. You have definite notions as to what is and what is not part of human nature and of the natural condition of mankind. Only the examination of anthropological facts can show whether those notions are or are not correct.

BRONISLAW MALINOWSKI
AND
ROBERT BRIFFAULT

BRONISLAW MALINOWSKI

AND

ROBERT BRIFFAULT

CHAPTER III

WHAT IS A FAMILY?

Bronislaw Malinowski: Last week, Briffault, you developed the theory of primitive mother-right, and you attacked the patriarchal point of view. Since, as you know, I am not a supporter of the Adam-and-Eve theory of marriage origins, nor yet an anti-feminist, I neither can, nor wish to, accept your challenge. But there was another point in your talk with which I definitely disagree, and there I am quite ready to join issue with you. All you said last time implies that individual marriage is a late invention—an artificial product. According to you, if I understand you rightly, the original domestic institution was a communal body—the maternal clan, based on group-marriage and on joint parenthood. I, on the other hand, unreservedly affirm that the individual family has always existed, and that it is invariably based on marriage in single pairs.

Robert Briffault: The word 'family' covers a variety of meanings, precisely because the conception and constitution of the family have undergone many changes. Family, in Latin *familia*, meant a man's goods and chattels, his man-servant and his maid-servant, his ox, his ass, and his wife. Or, again, when we say that the cat has a family, we are not referring to a group consisting of papa, mama and baby. Papa, as a matter of fact, is not there. The animal family consists essentially of mother and young. As I indicated last week, the primitive human family resembled the animal family more closely than does the civilised family. It consists essentially of mother and children. Only, there are several generations of mothers and children. Those accumulated generations constitute the maternal clan. The maternal clan, then, is a family. It is not a social or political institution consisting of associated families. The individual family of which you speak, that is the family consisting of papa, mama and baby, in other words the patriarchal family, does not exist side by side with the maternal clan. The latter takes its place and is just as much a family as the patriarchal family. As to its being monogamous, you know very well, Malinowski, that if I were to ask you to name a single undisputed instance of a monogamous savage tribe I would be placing you in an embarrassing position, and I have no wish to do that.

Malinowski: It depends on what you mean by 'monogamous marriage.' If by monogamy you understand the absolute rule that a man can have only one wife and a woman only one husband at a time—then this Christian and civilised monogamy is of late development. But marriage in single pairs—monogamy in the sense in which Westermarck and I are using it—is primeval, unless, that is, you assume the existence of group-marriage. I do not argue against the sporadic and rare occurrence of polygamy. I argue against the existence of communal or group-marriage. Now, polygamy, or plurality of wives, does not mean communal marriage. It, in fact, implies the existence of individual marriage.

Briffault: That's all very well, but you still seem to me to beg the question by using the phrase 'individual marriage' in an ambiguous sense. I think I must press you to a clearer definition of what you intend by individual marriage.

B.M.: By individual marriage I mean a legal contract between one man and one woman, guaranteeing to each mutual rights and obligations, and guaranteeing to the children a legal status. Polygamy, on such a definition of marriage, is a series of individual contracts. And it is the existence of individual marriage that you and your school are denying. I want to thrash out the question, then, whether marriage is essentially an individual contract, or, as you maintain, a state of group-relationship. In discussing this we touch on an issue of the greatest actuality and importance. I have shown that the fight in defence of marriage is nowadays on two fronts; parental communism versus the family, and sexual communism versus marriage. The communistic legislator objects to marriage, because marriage is, for him, a capitalistic institution, a sort of economic enslavement of woman. He is also out to undermine the individual influence of the home, that is, of the child's own parents, because to him the State, the Community, the Workers' Union ought to educate the future citizen from his early childhood. The modern Hedonist and Misbehaviourist is bent on destroying the home since this is to him the synonym of boredom and repression. To quote the words of a modern Misbehaviourist: 'Home is the place which does make idiots and lunatics of all of us.' The Misbehaviourist also believes that sex is 'for recreation and not for procreation.' He must, therefore, attack marriage and banish to a communal creche the occasional and accidental children. The anthropologist is, then, faced with a question: Is communal parenthood compatible with human nature and social order? I flatly deny that it is. You, on the other hand, uphold the possibility of group-marriage and group-parenthood. In your learned and brilliant work, *The Mothers,* you have given a renewed currency to the concept of communal parenthood, nay of group maternity. Let me quote your words: 'The clan, like the family, is a reproductive group.' And again you maintain that the clan is a 'group depending upon certain intimate relations, reproductive and economic'. And you are not alone. The great Cambridge anthropologist, Dr. Rivers has it in cold print: 'A child born into a community with clans becomes a member of a domestic group other than the family in the strict sense.' Now, to me, all this is Greek. You surely don't mean that the clan is really a reproductive group in the same sense as the family?

R. B.: I most certainly do. The maternal clan is, as I said before, a family group, not a group of families. The assumption that there can be no other form of family, no other reproductive group, than that consisting of papa, mama and baby will no doubt appear very natural to most people, but it is not scientific. The beehive, that extremely matriarchal group, is purely and solely a reproductive group and nothing else. It is a family, but it is not a patriarchal family. I go as far back as the bee-hive because by doing so we escape altogether from conventional and traditional definitions. The definition of what is a reproductive group is here given by nature herself, and she ought to know. I might adduce many other examples of family groups among animals constituted in the same way—of generations of mothers and young. The maternal clan which both you and I find to be the basis of social organisation in lower cultures is in the same manner a family, the foundation of kinship, that is, a reproductive group, not a social fiction. You may, to be sure, point out that the germs of the paternal or, as you say, the individual family, may be found at the present day in conjunction with maternal clans which, after thousands or perhaps millions of years, are no longer primitive. But I need not tell you that such individual associations do not represent the whole of the relation between men and women, for you have yourself amply illustrated the fact in your own researches. The organisation of the maternal clan regulates not only social relations in general, but also the relations between the sexes. It is, therefore, a reproductive group in the same sense as the hive of bees, or any other form of family, is a reproductive group.

B. M.: Let us leave the beehive on one side and concentrate on the human family. You define 'group-marriage' as 'a limitation of sexual freedom and promiscuity.' But this makes 'marriage' embrace all sorts of temporary and occasional relations. Now, to me, marriage is something infinitely bigger and more complicated than mere sexual relations. Marriage means to me a community of household, common work, and common interests; in short, a co-operative economic unity based on a legal contract and very often on religious and moral ideas. Marriage is thus to me a legal, economic, and often a religious institution associated as much with parenthood as with the personal relations between husband and wife. My view, then, implies that there can be no group-marriage without group-parenthood. Remember that Dr. Rivers, who first put forward the famous hypothesis of group-motherhood, suggested that its real home was in Melanesia. Now, for this very reason, in my own field work in Melanesia, I made a special study of motherhood. What did I find? There is no doubt at all that native custom, law and morals attach an immense importance to maternity. They surround motherhood with a whole set of moral and legal rules—we might almost speak of a religious cult of the mother. But this cult, far from communalising motherhood, makes it emphatically an individual

relationship. One woman and one woman only is bound
to the child which is of her body. These natives have
no strong views about pre-nuptial conduct. Yet, with
all this, if a girl is to become a mother she must be
married. So that society decrees that children must be
born in wedlock. They must have one mother. They
must also have one father. This is the more remarkable because these natives have no idea as to the phys-
iology of fatherhood. They believe that a spirit-ancestor
places a tiny baby in the mother's body where it devel-
ops.[1] Individual marriage once concluded, the wife is
allowed to become a mother and her husband is, by the
fact of marriage, recognized as the individual father.
Paternity is established by the contract of marriage.[2]
The existence of group-parenthood assumed by Rivers in
Melanesia we may dismiss as an exploded myth. There
is a story of an old lady in Cambridge who, hearing
about Dr. Rivers' theory of group-motherhood, philo-
sophically remarked: 'You can see at once that Dr.
Rivers has never been a mother himself!' Without
wishing to be personal, I would like to say the same
thing to you, Briffault. I spoke only about Melanesia, but
I am certain that every old woman in Asia, in the Malay
Archipelago, Australia, Africa, or in the South American jungle would endorse the wise criticism of the old
lady of Cambridge.

R. B.: That a man can have only one mother does
not prove that he can have only one wife. Your in-
genious argument no more proves that the Victorian
family is the prototype of human society than it proves
King Solomon to have been a monogamist. The Tro-

brianders, of whom you have made so admirable a study, are patriarchal, or well on the way to becoming so. The men have established patrilocal marriage, so far at least as to keep their children with them until puberty, when they return to the maternal clan and the protection of their maternal uncles. But it is quite impossible to generalise from one island to the whole of primitive humanity. Had you carried out your investigations in some other parts of the same region, not a hundred miles away, you might have come upon slightly different arrangements in which even the rudiments of patrilocal marriage and of paternal guardianship do not exist. I shall not adduce the opinion of any anthropologist, but the very words of a Papuan native called A. 'One of your wives will be a woman living in another village, B; another in C, a third wife in D, and so forth. No wife lives with you in your village, but it is your business to visit them in their villages. The children of those women belong to the village and to the tribe of their mothers, so that you have no children in your village. But your sister lives with you and a man from another village visits her. Her children are counted to your clan, not to his. Thus your own children stay in other tribes, but your sister's children live with you.' The savage child, before the establishment of patriarchal marriage, is thus certainly not born into the family of the father, but into the clan of his mother. The latter is a reality, the former has neither name nor existence. It has never occurred to any savage or to any anthropologist to suggest that a child is born from several mothers, though the savage does, as a matter of fact, call every one of his aunts 'mother.' But where marriage is purely matrilocal, his mother's relatives do look after the child and his father does not. The savage father is, in my experience, considerably fonder of children than is the average English father, but he does not regard them with a possessive feeling, and is equally fond of them whether they are or are not his progeny. Even should he take a more serious view of his parental obligations than do most civilised fathers, he is rigidly debarred by tribal law from fulfilling them. Those obligations devolve not on the father, but on the children's uncles. It is under the influence of their mother's peoples that they grow up, it is loyalty to them, not the honouring of their father and mother, which is inculcated by tribal tradition, by tribal ceremonies, by tribal organisation. Let me quote the words of another savage, an American Indian this time. 'You white people,' he said to a missionary, 'love your own children only. We love the children of the clan. They belong to all the people, and we care for them. They are bone of our bone, and flesh of our flesh. We are all father and mother to them. White people are savages; they do not love their children. If children are orphaned, people have to be paid to look after them. We know nothing of such barbarous ideas.' Kinship and affection are even closer ties in primitive, than in civilised society. But they are rooted in the maternal clan and not in the paternal family.[3] I do not say that the germs of the paternal family are nowhere to be found in societies which, at the present day, are no longer primitive. But they are overshadowed throughout uncultured humanity by the solidarity of the maternal clan, which is the only recognised social group, and are, therefore, the germs of a later growth.

B. M.: Some of what you said just now appears to me not quite relevant. The Papuan native, whom you quote, merely describes cases of multiple polygamy distributed over several villages. The fact that a man has several wives in different localities does not convert his wives into group-mothers. It still less makes him into a group of fathers. Moreover, a child born into a household occasionally visited by the father still remains born into his father's household and not into the maternal clan. Your statement from North America, on the other hand, is quite to the point. As it happens, I have spent some time among the most matriarchal Indians of North America, among the Hopi of Arizona. They talk about the brotherhood of the clan even as we Christians speak about the brotherhood of mankind, and it means precisely as much. It is possible to be too credulous even about what a native tells you. And again, you have taken King Solomon's testimony against me. He was certainly not a monogamist. Nor did I accuse him of it. But he was a wise man and, if you remember his judgment, it went dead against communal maternity. The most important link in my argument, however, is the question of group-maternity. You constantly spoke of the clan as a domestic institution; and this conception, I maintain, implies the existence of collective maternity. As in every individual family there is one mother who is the pivot of family life, so in this collective household there would have been a sort of 'collective mother,' that is, a group of mothers. On this group-motherhood I did harp constantly, but I think you failed to give us any clear instances. In fact, the hypothesis has been seriously advanced only with regard to Melanesia, and there, I can assure you, group maternity does not exist. And without group maternity, I maintain, there can be neither group marriage nor yet can the maternal clan be a domestic institution. Parenthood and, above all, maternity, is the pivotal point in the anatomy of marriage and family: on this you, Briffault, and I fully agree. We also agree that women will have the last word in deciding what the future of marriage is to be, even as they probably always had the first say in matters of love, marriage, and parenthood. Women now claim freedom. They want to share more fully in our national life, whether working in factories or in the professions, whether debating in Trade Union Councils or in Parliament. But women still have to become mothers and they still desire motherhood as deeply as any savages or any mid-Victorians. To us, as well as to most savages, love and playing at love is still clearly distinct from marriage. The savage makes love early in life and often experiments with infatuation and with sex. This is true also of the continental peasants, and also, to a large extent, of the wider masses in all European countries. I should say that a man in any country or at any level of culture marries when he wants children; or, more truly, perhaps, marries when his sweetheart desires to have children. And then the biggest tie between them comes into being. Now the question of the future is whether women will cease to be interested in maternity. If women still intend to keep up the vocation of maternity, will they still insist on carrying it on under the system of individual maternity, or will they prefer to give over the children to creches and communal institutions? Will a woman, however intelligent, feminist, or progressive, consent to undergo the hardships and dangers of childbirth in order to give over her child to a glorified foundlings' hospital or State incubator? Here again you know my answer: maternity is individual, has been individual, and will be the most individual of social forces. Finally, if woman is still to be a mother and an individual mother at that, will she choose to have her sweetheart as a mate and as a father to her children? Will she still desire him to stick to her and to share the responsibilities of parenthood? These three questions contain the essence of all marriage problems, past, present, and future. It is incorrect, I think, to regard the marriage contract as established mainly in the interests of the husband. It is quite as much at least a charter and a protection to the woman. Most men would consent to be drones easily enough; but no sound social order can allow them to do this. And here, I think, is the most fundamental point of the debate, namely, that marriage and family are based on the need of the male to face his responsibility and to take his share in the process of reproduction and of the continuity of culture. Another important issue is one of unlimited collectivism versus individualism. I think that the fairest answer will be that it is as incorrect to say that at any time of human development, past, present, or future, the human being can be exclusively a communist, as to maintain that he ever has been an exclusive individualist. Both forces are at play in marriage and the family as well as in economic organisation.

ROBERT
BRIFFAULT

ROBERT

BRIFFAULT

CHAPTER IV

THE BUSINESS SIDE OF MARRIAGE

Our Victorian grandmothers were—though the fact is apt to be overlooked—revolutionaries. At the beginning of the nineteenth century, when the bold ideas of the French Revolution were still thick in the air, the more intelligent among our grandmothers revolted against the attitude which had been prevalent that marriage was purely a social and sordidly economic arrangement—so much dowry against so much income. Our intelligent grandmothers were great novel readers. And the usual theme of the Victorian novel was the triumph of love over lucre. That was a quite revolutionary idea, and scandalized many old gentlemen in those days. Up to that time there had been a notion in

English society—and to a far greater extent in continental society—that a love-match was a rather scandalous thing and certainly not quite respectable. Such an event gave rise to a considerable amount of whispering behind fans. Victorian sentiment constituted a bold and subversive revolution in the general attitude towards marriage. We find the attitude of early Victorian old gentlemen repeated among the Negroes of the Gold Coast. In a court of law there it was argued lately by the Negro Counsel for the prosecution that a certain couple were not really and respectably married and that their children could not be regarded as legitimate; for the couple, the lawyer alleged, had married for love. That is regarded in most savage societies as a very scandalous state of affairs, but the sentiments of decency of savages are not often subjected to such an outrage, for the occurrence is extremely unusual.

When an Australian black is asked why he marries, which he does when he is getting on in years and is thinking of retiring from the more active pursuits of life, he answers that he requires a wife to fetch sticks for his fire, to cook his dinner, and to attend to his household arrangements generally. He does not say that he marries her because he loves her or because his instincts demand it. Those reasons would be absurd. The first because his notions of romance are very rudimentary, and the second because there is not the slightest occasion for him to marry in order to satisfy his instincts.[1]

If, following out the various forms of the institution of marriage, we work our way up from the Australian

black, through the various stages in the evolution of
culture, glancing at the matrimonial arrangements of
African chiefs, or Chinese mandarins, up to those of a
French peasant or of an English duke, we shall find in
every quarter of the globe and in every age that the
transaction rests chiefly, and in most instances exclusively,
upon economic considerations.[2] The reason why an
English duke marries is not quite the same as that for
which the Australian black marries. The noble duke
does not require a duchess in order that she may cook
his dinner. But he requires her in order that he shall
have an heir to whom he may hand down the estate
and who shall carry on the family name and traditions.

I do not wish you to think that I am taking a
cynical and materialistic view. Nowadays the most
common motive leading to marriage is, I believe, falling in love. But here again it would be a great mistake
to apply to the lower stages of culture the sentiments
of our own society. Our reports and observations about
savages are very emphatic and uniform as to the absence of romantic love amongst them.[3] Now, knowing
how very prone we are ourselves to fall in love, we may
find it difficult to understand those statements and we
may consider that if anything is part of human nature,
surely this is. We find it difficult to realise the effects
of different social conditions on human nature. This is
where anthropology comes in. We live under strictly
individualistic conditions in which every man's interests
are more or less threatened by the antagonistic interests of other people. Human beings are, I firmly
believe, naturally sympathetic, affectionate, and kind

hearted. But the social conditions of individual competition do not allow of their sympathy and kind hearts running away with them. We have to be on our guard. It is very seldom that we can afford to trust another human being completely. Civilised man is essentially lonely. To be released from that necessity of being on our guard, to be able to trust another human being, in other words, to be loved, is in those circumstances one of the deepest cravings of human nature. And that craving, the result of our essential loneliness, has become in our cultures intimately blended with the relation between man and woman. The conditions are quite different in primitive uncultured society. The savage is never lonely. His social unit, the clan, is a big family. And, just as in a harmonious big family, there are not the acute conflicts of interests which compel civilised man to be on his guard and make him lonely. Consequently among savages, who are every bit as affectionate as we are, affection is not concentrated on the man-woman relation; it is diffused in the comradeship of the clan. The savage, as a general rule, is quite kind and tender to his women. But no more so to his wife than to his mother or sisters or his brothers or children of the clan. The most definite and unanimous testimonies which we have of affection between man and woman among savages refer to the devotion between very old married couples. In other words, love among savages is the result, rather than the cause of marriage. Which, by the way, seems to me a very sensible and satisfactory state of things.

The patriarchal privileges which modern women are disposed to resent are founded in the last resort upon economic advantages. They are not founded upon the possession by men of superior physical force or superior brains, but in the possession of a superior banking account. The dependence of woman in patriarchal society is an economic dependence. That economic advantage of men is not necessarily the outcome of superior ingenuity, but is the result of the division of labour between the sexes. One very definite reason why patriarchal society cannot be supposed to represent the primeval condition of the human race is that such an economic dependence of the women and economic monopoly of the men does not exist in the lower phases of culture. Far from the men possessing the advantage of a superior banking account, it is, on the contrary, the women who are the producers of every form of primitive wealth.[4]

Where the women remain after marriage in their own home and among their people, and the husband joins them there, the children belong to their mother's clan. A child is not the heir to his father's property or to his name, he derives both from his mother and from her relatives.[5] One consequence of that organisation and that form of marriage, which we call matrilocal, is that there are no illegitimate children. The term illegitimate has no meaning in the lower cultures.[6] It has no meaning where marriage is matrilocal and a child takes its mother's, not its father's name. There were no illegitimate children in ancient Japan, in ancient Egypt. There were none among the plebeians in ancient Rome. All children being members of their mother's clan, and not of their father's family, are equally legitimate and no legal contract of any kind, no religious ceremony is required to make them so. A legal contract is required to make a child legitimate only where he must inherit his father's name and property.

Among many people, such as the Samoans there are very elaborate marriage contracts and ceremonies, but only in the case of chiefs and owners of important property. The common and poor people, although they may bring up large families, are not said to marry, but to live at their pleasure in concubinage. Among the native peons of Mexico a marriage contract seldom takes place. They bring up large families of illegitimate children. They are at the present day Roman Catholics. But they are habitually content to live in sin and rear families of bastards. It does not matter to them; they have no property to transmit. It is only where property is at stake that the legitimacy of marriage, the legitimacy of the children comes to be of importance.[7] A legitimate child is one capable of inheriting property from his father, and a legitimate wife is one who can be the mother of a legitimate heir.

The old doctrine that primitive humanity is monogamous is not true in the least. But it is true that polygamy[8] is not extensive where the people are poor, where economic conditions, as among forest tribes, are wretched. When we rise to stages of culture where the men possess considerable wealth, which happens for the first time in pastoral societies, we find that polygamy is universal and extensive. It is in pastoral societies, and in

the civilisations which have developed out of them that
the exuberant harems of Africa and the Orient flourish.

It has been otherwise in the cradles of European
culture, in Greece, in Italy. There the people have never
been purely pastoralists. The land is too broken. The
Greeks were agriculturists from the first. And the land
belonged to the women who were the original agricul-
tural labourers. The object of the legal contract was in
Greek law, to transfer the land vested in the woman to
her husband's children. Men married women and their
land, that is, their dowry. A woman without a dowry
could not get married. In those conditions there could
be no plurality of legitimate wives. Monogamy was
imposed by the economic situation, and thus became the
legal form of contract of Western culture, as opposed to
the legal polygamy of the pastoralist societies of the
East. The development of European patriarchal monogamy, of the patriarchal family, of monogamic sentiment
and morality, is thus the outcome of economic conditions. Those institutions and those sentiments were imposed by Christianity upon our savage ancestors. The
Anglo-Saxon synod of 786 decreed that 'the son of a
meretricious union shall be debarred from legally inheriting, for in accordance with the apostolic authority
of holy decrees, we regard adulterine children as spurious.
We command then that every layman shall have one
legitimate wife and every woman one legitimate husband in order that they may have and beget legitimate
heirs according to God's law.' Thus were our marriage
institutions established in England in the form in which
they obtain at the present day.

The danger of overlooking the fact that those institutions are the product of a long evolution and have undergone many changes lies in the delusion that once marriages have been made in Heaven they can be left to Heaven's care. There is no more common cause of disaster than that anthropological fallacy. There is another kind of danger. To accept the authority of mere tradition as such is no less blind and disastrous than to reject its products indiscriminately merely because they are 'artificial.' The tradition of our marriage institutions contains many relics of modern intelligence on the mere authority of an ancient tradition. Tradition hands down the good and the evil inextricably combined. It has no authority to discriminate between them. To sift the gold from the dross in our cultural legacy is the part of equity and intelligence. Marriage and the family have in the course of cultural evolution been many different things in turn. The present crisis which that evolution is undergoing will undoubtedly result in many changes, and has already done so. Those changes must needs be in the direction of eliminating the elements of arbitrary coercion from the most personal of relations and of making it more and more a private contract. You will be told by many people that the modification in our attitude towards the relations between men and women endangers the sanctity of that relation. The reverse is, I maintain, the case. The substitution of intelligence for the authority of tradition endangers the tragedy of unhappy marriages. It endangers nothing else; it makes, on the contrary, the realisation of the ideal of marriage more attainable than it could ever have been before. Marriage has rested upon instincts, it has rested upon economic conditions, it has rested upon traditional and romantic sentiments. It is to be hoped that it will rest in the future to a larger extent than in the past upon intelligence and justice.

BRONISLAW
MALINOWSKI

BRONISLAW

MALINOWSKI

CHAPTER V

MARRIAGE AS A RELIGIOUS

INSTITUTION

Marriage is regarded in all human societies as a
sacrament, that is, as a sacred transaction establishing a
relationship of the highest value to man and woman.
In treating a vow or an agreement as a sacrament, society
mobilises all its forces, legal as well as moral, to cement
a stable union.

There is no doubt that the most primitive peoples
as well as those highly developed do regard marriage as
a sacrament. It has to be solemnised at sacred seasons or
days; and it is usually contracted at hallowed or specially
appropriate places—in churches or temples, in the public
place of a village, or before the gods of the domestic
hearth. Bride and bridegroom have to purify themselves

spiritually and bodily. They have to dress in clothes with a religious or magical significance.

The wedding rite itself has invariably a magical or a religious character. In most ceremonies the symbolism expresses the traditional view that in marriage bride and bridegroom are firmly united by a sacred bond. The joining of hands or fingers, the tying of garments, the exchange of rings and chains—so familiar to us from our own civilisation—are practised throughout the world. Usually not merely the two consorts, nor even only the families of bride and bridegroom, but the whole community are drawn in.

I have given you here a brief summary of what the wedding ceremony is—a summary which holds good for all peoples of the world: the pigmies of the Indian Ocean, the Australian aborigines, the South Sea islanders, the Indians of the New World, the natives of Africa and of Asia, and, as you know, the inhabitants of Europe. Through all this, marriage is made public and solemn. It is the announcement to all and sundry that an important legal transaction has taken place. The magical and religious form, again, which is inherent in the sacramental rite shows how deeply human beings are moved by marriage, how much they apprehend from the dangers which beset it, and how deeply they feel that they have to rely on a higher supernatural assistance.

But the point which is of the greatest importance for my argument is that the sacrament of marriage has always an exclusive and individual character. There is not one single instance of a group wedding, of a religious sacrament performed to unite a group of women with a group of men, and thus to give moral and religious sanction to a state of group promiscuity. The notion of a promiscuous group wedding has on its face the stigma of absurdity. This is why the advocates of group marriage, past, present or future, always underrate the scientific importance of the sacramental or religious side of marriage.

THE NEED OF SANCTIONS

The legal and religious sanctioning of marriage, which is so conspicuous among the primitives, is still the question which agitates the reformers and moralists of to-day. Are we to secularise marriage completely and withdraw it from the control of religion, and perhaps even of law, as is the tendency in Soviet legislation and in the programme of many would-be reformers? Here the anthropologist comes in and tells you that throughout primitive humanity we find a very strong emphasis on both the legal and the religious sides of individual marriage. Is this not an indication that there must be a profound need of tribal and supernatural sanctions given to the matrimonial relationship?

I think the answer will have to be in the affirmative. Some enthusiastic Misbehaviourists of to-day, with all their spurious apparatus of anthropological conjecture, would like us to believe that monogamy, religion and morality are a mid-Victorian invention. True scientific anthropology teaches us another lesson. Individual marriage sanctioned by religion as well as by law exists throughout humanity, primitive and civilised alike.

But, you might interpose here, the wedding ceremony just starts marriage, endows its beginnings with solemnity and pomp—but then, once the wedding is over, marriage becomes an essentially secular, humdrum relation. This is not true of our own religious conception of marriage, which, once a sacrament, remains always a sacrament. Marriage, it is said, 'was ordained for the procreation of children, to be brought up in the fear and nurture of the Lord, and to the praise of His Holy Name.' Now this, in a way, is true of every human community; for the procreation of children as well as their bringing-up, is to most primitive peoples a religious matter. The fact of conception is usually associated with spiritual and supernatural ideas. Conception is regarded as the reincarnation of ancestor-spirits by the natives of Central Australia, by many Melanesians, by West African Negroes, by the Bantu, and by many Indians. The coming of life links man with the world of supernatural beings. Accordingly, when pregnancy sets in, husband and wife have to submit to ritual observances and restrictions.

Birth, again, is invariably a tabooed and ceremonial occasion. There are the ritual lustrations of mother and child, the naming of the child, its reception into the tribe, into the community of the believers. Marriage is kept at a sacramental pitch in the hallowing of gestation, of parenthood and of education. The family becomes a religious unit.

BRONISLAW MALINOWSKI

The Insoluble Link

We repeat in our own marriage service the solemn words, 'for better for worse, for richer for poorer, in sickness and in health, to love and to cherish till death us do part.' But, impressive and final as this is, it would not be enough to a great many peoples. For to many whom we regard as savages or barbarians, not even death can part husband and wife. The widow sacrifices herself or is sacrificed at her husband's grave, and that not only in India but also in Peru, in West Africa, among the Bantu, in Fiji, in the New Hebrides and the Solomon Islands, and in New Zealand. And in all communities it is the bereft consort, the widow or widower, who has to keep the deepest and most burdensome mourning, who has at times to be sacramentally divorced from the spirit of the deceased; the tie which had united the survivor to the dead one, the tie of marriage, is stronger even than death itself.

Primitive Love

But the real importance of religious ritual is in that it expresses strong moral sentiment; the sacrament which binds two people means that these two people stand in a very intimate moral relationship. There is nothing more important to realise with regard to the institution of marriage than that it is everywhere based on love and affection. One of the most dehumanising anthropological fallacies is the notion that the savage knows no real love, that he is incapable of falling in love. Many people who write books on anthropology will tell you that romantic love was invented a few generations ago—will tell you almost that it was invented by Queen Victoria and Prince Albert.

I maintain that among the most primitive peoples, real love, the blend of physical attraction and appreciation of personality, does exist and that many primitive marriages are based on such love. I have myself observed it in the South Seas, among the North American Indians, as well as among the Eastern and Central European peasants in slightly different forms and shades, but still the genuine article.

In most human societies there exists an almost mystical bond of mutual dependence between husband and wife. The notion is universal that the honour and success of the husband depend upon his wife's conduct, while the welfare of the wife is determined by what the husband does. In the traditional ethics of Europe, the wife's misconduct brings dishonour on the husband—a dishonour which, according to the ethics of duelling, can only be washed in blood. To the savages a similar notion tells that the wife's adultery may have fatal or, at any rate, dangerous consequences for the husband. When the Dyaks are on a head-hunting expedition, the unchastity of the wife kills her husband. On the big overseas expeditions of the South Sea Trobriand Islanders, strict chastity was obligatory to the wives at home, or else the whole crew of a canoe might be drowned. It is when the husband is in peril that the wife must not only be faithful to him, but also carry out a whole series of magical rites and observances on his behalf. And again, it is when the wife is ill, above all when she is pregnant and in childbed, that the husband has to be chaste and carry out a number of strict observances.

In many communities husband and wife keep their religions separate, each worshipping his or her own line of ancestral gods or guardian spirits; but each has to show respect for the other's cult. So we see that in all communities the unity of matrimonial relations is watched over and enforced by super-natural powers.

But the deeper reason for this is that such an intimate co-operation cannot work except it be based on strong mutual attachment. 'He that loveth his wife loveth himself,' is at the same time the highest ethical rule and the most adequate expression of self-interest. And it is that because it expresses the supreme sociological wisdom.

A Personal Sacrament

In establishing the religious side of marriage I want to show once more the immense cultural importance of this relationship, and the depths to which it is founded in human culture and tradition. As we have seen, the religious sanctions embrace the legal character of marriage, that is, they make it binding, public and enforced by the organised interests of the community. In proving that individual marriage is a sacrament I am able to show you that marriage is a binding contract between one man and one woman for the establishment of an individual family.

In this argument there is contained one of the most convincing disprovals of group marriage: for, we have seen, the primitive sacrament of marriage is as personal and as individual as our own marriage service. Parenthood, again, and especially motherhood, is, in its religious setting, emphatically individual. Group motherhood—of which there is not one single authenticated instance on record—we can discard as an unwarranted hypothesis.

The main function of religion is to standardise those sentiments and relationships which have a fundamental value for mankind. Individual marriage has been thus hall-marked as an indispensable institution from the outset. Strict monogamy has been the goal toward which the religious as well as the legal conception of marriage has been steadily advancing.

The fact that marriage, throughout humanity is a religious institution proves, then, above all that marriage is an extremely valuable institution. But it is an institution which can be maintained only at great personal sacrifice of husband and wife. On this point I am glad to be in complete agreement with Dr. Briffault.

I trust also that you appreciate that I am not speaking about the religious side of marriage in the spirit of sanctimoniousness. For I cannot honestly identify myself with any one religious point of view. In my case it would be sheer hypocrisy. But I firmly believe that the majority of people of our present civilisation are, in one way or another, religious. So let them keep their religious marriage. Even in Russia most marriages are, I am informed, still solemnised in church as well as before the registrar.

But what about the many people in this country, as elsewhere, who are frankly Agnostic, that is, do not subscribe to any positive religion? Here the most important thing to grasp is that Agnosticism does not and must not mean the absence of moral values. The Agnostic has his sacred things and his sacramental relations, though he does not create them by means of the rites of an established creed. Now, by scientific analysis, we have arrived at the conviction that marriage is of the highest importance for any healthy and progressive society. The Agnostic, whose main moral foundation is laid down by reason and science, will not aim at the destruction or even at the undermining of institutions. On the contrary, he must endow the institution of marriage and the family with new values, and so make them stable and sacred in his own fashion.

In showing you that the tradition of individual marriage and family has its roots in the deepest needs of human nature and of social order, I have contributed my share to what might be called the lay, or scientific consecration of marriage.

BRONISLAW
MALINOWSKI

BRONISLAW
MALINOWSKI

CHAPTER VI
PERSONAL PROBLEMS

What have we learnt from this symposium on marriage? My task is to focus the bewildering variety of facts, arguments—I might say, almost, of sentiments —which has been put before you.

POINTS OF AGREEMENT

I shall not dwell on the points of disagreement between Dr. Briffault and myself; they have given you a good insight into the famous anthropological disputes about the origin of marriage. The points of disagreement do not matter so very much as regards modern practical questions.

But out of the discussion there have emerged clearly one or two points of agreement, and these, I think, are very illuminating as the background for discussions of present-day difficulties. In the first place there was substantial agreement as to the complexity and manifoldness of marriage. You have seen that marriage is not merely a state of sexual relationship, but that it implies a common household, joint parenthood, and a great deal of economic co-operation. Marriage, as I have insisted throughout, is essentially a legal contract which usually enjoys also definite religious, that is supernatural, sanctions. As a matter of fact, the worst errors in the theory of marriage have arisen from the confusion between the legally binding, economically founded, religiously sanctioned institution of marriage on the one hand, and casual and temporary intrigues on the other. Among the New Guinea natives whom I have studied, boys and girls are allowed by custom to go through a series of more or less serious love affairs, settling down finally to a lasting liaison which eventually becomes transformed into marriage by the legal act of wedding. And this is a type of conduct which we find repeated in many other communities all the world over. Now, such temporary liaisons, which often take place in special communal houses, have led superficial observers to speak about the existence of actual cases or 'survivals' of group-marriage. Nothing could be more misleading, for the relationship which obtains between the boys and girls is absolutely different from marriage, and is clearly distinguished from marriage by the natives.

The second point on which there was a consensus of opinion was the value of maternity in all questions of marriage and parenthood. I personally am deeply convinced that from the very beginning it was woman who, as the mother, had the greatest influence on the forms of marriage, of the household, and of the management of children. At the same time, all my studies of primitive mankind, all my personal experiences among savages and civilised people, have convinced me that maternal affection is individual. And it is because of that, I believe, that the family and marriage from the beginnings were individual. You will remember that I laid great emphasis on the fact that maternity is individual. A whole school of anthropologists, from Bachofen on, have maintained that the maternal clan was the primitive domestic institution, and that, connected with this, there was group marriage or collective marriage. In my opinion, as you know, this is entirely incorrect. But an idea like that, once it is taken seriously and applied to modern conditions, becomes positively dangerous. I believe that the most disruptive element in the modern revolutionary tendencies is the idea that parenthood can be made collective. If once we came to the point of doing away with the individual family as the pivotal element of our society, we should be faced with a social catastrophe compared with which the political upheaval of the French revolution and the economic changes of Bolshevism are insignificant. The question, therefore, as to whether group motherhood is an institution which ever existed, whether it is an arrangement which is compatible with human nature and social order, is of considerable practical interest.

CLAN AND SEX

Now on this point I can be quite dogmatic. The hypothesis of group maternity has been seriously advanced by a real anthropologist, the late Dr. Rivers of Cambridge, only with regard to Melanesia. This is, in fact, the only part of the world where there were some indications that it might have existed. But having spent several years there and made special observations on this point, I can now state positively that there is not even the slightest semblance of collective maternity there. You will notice that in our debate on the subject, Dr. Briffault was not even prepared to reaffirm the existence of group maternity. In his important work *The Mothers,* on the other hand, where he exposes his views so brilliantly, group marriage and group maternity form the twofold foundation of his whole argument. And, indeed, the two are essentially connected, so that if you throw overboard group maternity you must also recant the idea of group marriage, because since parenthood, as I have tried to show you, is the essence of marriage, any form of group marriage would necessarily involve the existence of group maternity. After the present recantation, then, we can perhaps assume that it is impossible to regard the clan as the primeval domestic institution.

The clans, mind you, do exist and they are extremely important to the natives. But they fulfill special functions entirely different from those of the family, and they have nothing to do with domestic life or procreation. The only relation between clan and sex consists in the fact that membership in the same clan bars a man and a woman from marrying each other, or even from courtship. This, of course, does not make the clan into a family.

What bearing has this on modern conditions?

WOMAN'S CHOICE

If maternity has always been the central element of marriage, the inference is that in the future women will also have the last word in deciding what marriage is to be. Therefore, there are three crucial questions which the history of primitive marriage presents to the women of the future. Will women cease to be interested in becoming and being mothers, or on the contrary, will the maternal instinct remain as strong as ever? This is the first question. The second is: will the mothers of the future prefer to carry out individual maternity and continue looking after their own children, or will they try to call into being the hypothetical primeval clan, that is, will they give over their infants into the hands of the State to be brought up as foundlings or communal babies? In the third place, will the mother of the future desire to have the father of her child as her mate and husband, or will she prefer him to be a drone? You know my answer to every one of these questions. I believe that no human impulse is so deeply rooted as the maternal impulse in woman; I believe that it is individual;

and I believe that it is bound up with the institution of marriage.

The only example of real group maternity I heard of was from a farmer friend of mine; he had three geese who decided to sit communally on a nest of eggs. The result was that all the eggs were smashed in the quarrels and fights of this maternal clan of group mothers. All, that is, but one; the gosling, however, did not survive the tender cares of its group mothers. If ever another group of geese were to try a similar experiment I should like them to be aware of this precedent.

PATERNAL RESPONSIBILITY

It is a distortion of the truth to attack marriage on the plea that it is an enslavement of woman by man. The analysis of primitive marriage I gave you shows that marriage is a contract safeguarding the interests of the woman as well as granting privileges to man. A detailed study of the economic aspects of marriage reveals, in fact, that the man has to prove his capacity to maintain the woman. Often, as among the Siberian natives and certain African races and American Indians, the man has to reside with his parents-in-law for some time before marriage in order to prove that he is capable of maintaining his future wife and her offspring.

The laws of marriage and family express, among other things, the demand that the male should face his responsibility and should take his share of the duties and burdens as well as of the privileges connected with the process of reproduction.

A Personal Contract

Anthropology teaches us two things; marriage and the family have changed; they have developed; they have grown and passed through various stages. But, through all the changes and vicissitudes of history and development, the family and marriage still remain the same twin institution; they still emerge as a stable group showing throughout the same characteristics: the group consisting of father and mother and their children, forming a joint household, co-operating economically, legally united by a contract and surrounded by religious sanctions which make the family into a moral unit.

Every society, then, teaches its members the two matrimonial commandments. The one given to the males is: if you want to possess a wife of your choice and have children with her, you will have to shoulder your share of duties and burdens. The one for the woman is: if you want to become a mother you must stick to the lover of your choosing and do your duty by him as your husband as well as by your children.

Do these anthropological conclusions profoundly modify our outlook on present and future questions? Certainly. In the first place, we do feel a considerable diffidence as regards any ambitious reforms aiming at either the destruction, or a complete re-creation, of the family by means of external coercion and legislative changes on a vast scale. The reforms of Fascist Italy and of Soviet Russia alike will, I am convinced, lead to the same result: a return to the old order of marriage and family based neither on absolute freedom nor on complete and rigid compulsion.

You can see that I am not an alarmist. I do not seriously entertain any fears or doubts as to the future of marriage or the family. On the other hand, I sincerely deprecate the mere stubbornness of the moral reactionary, who refuses to see any dangerous symptoms in our present conditions and who does not want even the form of marriage and the family changed, who opposes any discussion on divorce or family limitation or on the 'revolt of modern youth.' This attitude works against the cause of true conservatism, that is, of wise reform.

ROOM FOR IMPROVEMENT

The institution of marriage shows symptoms of maladjustment, as do all other institutions, for the simple reason that we are living in an epoch of rapid and profound change in the whole structure of our civilisation. Thus a wide range of knowledge and constant stimulus given to imagination and emotion have made the modern young men and women much more alive to the need of the full sexual and erotic life. Those who believe in the institution of marriage must work not at the belittling of sex, but at showing that its full attainment can only be in a life-long relationship contracted for the fulfillment of all that sex can give, and also of all its consequences. Here I think that the work of such big educational organisations as the British Social Hygiene Council, who spread enlightenment and knowledge on moderate, but progressive, lines, is of the greatest importance. The eugenics movement, again, teaches us above all that love and the falling in love is not merely a phase in human life, but a matter of the greatest moment for the future of the human race. Such movements, then, will contribute towards the establishment of the marriage relationship, the basis of knowledge and of consideration for human needs.

How far we can attempt to create a science of love and love-making without becoming somewhat ridiculous and futile it is difficult to see. If any ultra-modern university were to establish a Chair of Domestic Happiness or of Scientific Love-Making, I should not apply for the incumbency. But there is no doubt, however, that the pioneering work of recent contributors to the scientific study of sex are of the greatest value.

Among some other actual problems connected with marriage let me mention divorce. Here I am all for progressive reconstruction. As to family limitation, let me just remind you of the statement of the Lambeth Conference: 'in those cases where there is a reason clearly for the moral obligation to limit or avoid parenthood and where there is a morally sound reason for avoiding complete abstinence . . . other methods may be used.' The Lambeth Conference has once and for all shut the mouth of those who maintain that Christianity is incompatible with the methods of birth control, in certain cases at least.

On the whole there is nothing as important and hopeful in this question as the progressive movement on the part of conservative agencies such as the Church of England or other Christian organisations. Nor is there anything as dangerous as to identify the cause of free thought and progress with a destructive attack against marriage, with Misbehaviourism and the futile and cheap attacks against the Christian influence on marriage, attacks which have been becoming lamentably frequent in the last few years.

SACRIFICE AND SAFEGUARDS

Marriage, I conclude, presents one of the most difficult personal problems in human life; the most emotional as well as the most romantic of all human dreams has to be consolidated into an ordinary working relationship which, while it begins by promising a supreme happiness, demands in the end the most unselfish and sublime sacrifices from man and woman alike. Marriage will never be a matter of living happily ever after. Marriage and the family are the foundations of our present society, as they were the foundations of all human societies. To maintain these foundations in good order is the duty of everyone. Each must contribute his individual share, while the social reformer and legislator must constantly watch over the institution as a whole. Because, as all things alive, marriage has to grow and change. Wise and moderate reforms—reforms, however, which may go deep towards modifying the institution—are necessary in order to prevent disastrous revolutionary upheavals.

ASHLEY
MONTAGU

ASHLEY
MONTAGU

NOTES

INTRODUCTION

1. By far the best account of Briffault's literary temperament, and, indeed, one of the best critical evaluations of *The Mothers,* is from the pen of Havelock Ellis. This is a review of the latter work in *The Birth Control Review* (New York), September 1928—reprinted in Havelock Ellis, *Views and Reviews,* Harmsworth, London, 1932, pp. 160-171. Briffault refers to this review, and makes contemptuous reference to Ellis, in his novel *Europa in Limbo,* Scribner's, New York, 1937, p. 47. In the novel Briffault disguises the work as a collaborative study with "Sir Anthony Fisher." "Old Haverstock Wallace [Havelock Ellis], the authority on depravity, who had himself suffered formerly from English covert censorship, went out of his way to review the book with much condescension in a sheet devoted to the advertisement of rubber goods, and deplored the 'predilection for the paradoxical which handicapped the authors'

literary temperament.' " Malinowski was caricatured in the
following words: "Professor Bronislawski, who had obtained much honor in England by proving the accuracy
of the story of Noah's Ark, and had been appointed in
consequence to the chair of Natural History in the University of Aldwych [The London School of Economics
at which Malinowski was first lecturer, then reader, and
eventually Professor], was particularly combatant. The
book, he said, was dangerous to public welfare, sapping as
it did the foundations of national patriotism in racial
heredity and the family. He approached the Home Secre-
tary and Archbishop of York with a view to having the
work suppressed on grounds of immorality. The *New
Statement* [*The New Statesman and Nation*] stated that
'Professor Bronislawski has once and for all disposed of
Sir Anthony Fisher's and Mr. Bern's puerilities.' Sir Anthony was, shortly after, dismissed from his lectureship
at Cambridge and his post at the Marine Biological Station."
2. A. R. Wallace, in Introductory Note to E. Westermarck,
The History of Human Marriage, vol. I, pp. ix sq.
3. Westermarck devoted half a book to a rebuttal of Briffault's
charges. See Edward Westermarck in " 'The Mothers,' A Re-
joinder to Dr. Briffault," *Three Essays on Sex and Marriage*,
Macmillan, London and New York, 1934, pp. 163-335. See
also Edward Westermarck, *The Future of Marriage in Western Civilization*, Macmillan, London and New York, 1936.
4. For the full development of Briffault's views the interested
reader is urged to read Briffault's work *The Mothers*, 3 vols.,
Allen & Unwin, London; Macmillan, New York, 1927, or
the statement of his essential thesis in the one-volume
work *The Mothers*, Macmillan, New York, 1931. For a
brief account of Briffault's work see Huntington Cairns,
"Robert Briffault and the Rehabilitation of the Matriarchal
Theory," in Harry Elmer Barnes (editor), *An Introduction
to the History of Sociology*, University of Chicago Press,
Chicago, 1948, pp. 668-676.
5. What Briffault thought of women may be read in *The
Mothers*, vol. 3, pp. 507-508: "It has been said that a man
learns nothing after forty; it may be said in the same broad
sense that a woman learns nothing after twenty-five."

6. A form of multiple marriage exists among the Kaingang of Brazil and the Toda of Southern India, but this is not to be confused with the 'group marriage' of Briffault's theory.
7. For a further discussion of this subject see M. J. Herskovits, *Economic Anthropology*, Knopf, New York, 1952.
8. For this evidence see M. F. Ashley Montagu, *The Direction of Human Development*, Harper and Bros., New York, 1955.
9. See G. P. Murdock, *Social Structure*, Macmillan, New York, 1949.
10. *Ibid.*, pp. 24, 25. Indeed, the theory of group-marriage is today as outmoded as the belief in the mythical Amazons, who are, nevertheless, often quoted in un-anthropological circles as *the* example of a matriarchal state and were so referred to by Briffault (*The Mothers*, vol. 1, p. 457). Since the Amazons never existed, but are a mythical group first mentioned by Herodotus and soon doubted by Strabo, their social organization need not further detain us, except perhaps as an enduring example of the will to believe.
11. Jules Henry, *Jungle People*, Augustin, New York, 1941.
12. For good accounts of the kibbutzim, see Melford Spiro, *Kibbutz*, Harvard University Press, Cambridge, 1956, and Esther Tauber, *Molding Society to Man*, Bloch, New York, 1955, pp. 70-81.
13. W. E. Goode, *After Marriage*, Free Press, Glencoe, Illinois, 1956.

CHAPTER 2

1. This is incorrect. Only about one-seventh of the investigated non-literate peoples are characterized by matrilocal residence. For example, among 250 societies investigated, 146 were found to be patrilocal, 38 matrilocal, 22 matri-patrilocal, 19 bilocal, 17 neolocal, and 8 avunculolocal. See George P. Murdock, *Social Structure*, Macmillan, New York, 1949, p. 17.
2. I do not know of an anthropologist who today would subscribe to such a view. As Murdock writes, "On the contrary, since the ancestors of nearly all groups which have survived

until today must have undergone many changes in social organization during the long course of human history, the fact that the last transition in a particular series has been from matrilineal to patrilineal or double descent by no means implies that the matrilineate came first in the entire series." *Op. cit.,* p. 219.

3. This statement, and those which follow, are incorrect. Matrilocal residence is more often than not associated with matrilineal inheritance. But there are many matrilocal societies in which inheritance is patrilineal, and some in which it is mixed. In many such societies, moreover, there are often distinct rules of inheritance for different types of property as well as for different kinds of succession to positions of status and authority.

CHAPTER 3

1. See Bronislaw Malinowski, *The Sexual Life of Savages in North Western Melanesia,* Harcourt, Brace, New York, 1929
2. For an exposition of this fact see Bronislaw Malinowski, *The Family Among the Australian Aborigines,* University of London Press, London, 1913. See also M. F Ashley Montagu, *Coming into Being among the Australian Aborigines,* Routledge, London, 1937, Dutton, New York, 1938.
3. This is, of course, patently untrue. Kinship and affection are quite as deeply rooted in paternal clan and family.

CHAPTER 4

1. This is not so. It was, in fact, difficult for the young Australian aboriginal male to satisfy his "instincts" because the older men usually married the available younger women.
2. Not at all. Marriage is only occasionally a matter that rests chiefly upon economic considerations.
3. This is far from true. Romantic love is a state known to affect the relations between the sexes in many non-literate societies. See, for example, Malinowski's *The Sexual Life of Savages.*
4. Something of an exaggeration. In non-literate societies men produce all sorts of valuable objects and accumulations of wealth.

5. It has already been stated that this is not true for all societies.
6. This is not so. In many non-literate societies a child must have a father, otherwise it is "illegitimate," and often, under such circumstances, both mother and child or the child alone will be killed. See M. F. Ashley Montagu, *Coming into Being among the Australian Aborigines.*
7. Not at all. In a good many societies a child cannot be fitted into the structure of society if the clan and moiety membership of the father is not known. Hence, an "illegitimate" child poses an insoluble problem to such societies, so that a "father" must be found for the child or it must be disposed of.
8. Briffault here means "polygyny" or culturally permitted marriage of one man with several women.